M11

New
Vestry Prayers

By

Rev. John L. Forster

MOORLEY'S Print & Publishing

British Library Cataloguing in Publication Data.
A catalogue record for this book is available
from the British Library.

MOORLEY'S Print & Publishing
23 Park Rd., Ilkeston, Derbys DE7 5DA
Tel/Fax: (0115) 932 0643

ISBN 0 86071 527 2

Foreword

Most preachers will tell you that the last few minutes before a service of worship begins are very important and very precious. All the preparation is complete and the moment approaches when you will lead the worship of the people of God.

The Church Vestry can be a very busy place as a sort of hub around which the activities of the Church revolve at service time. Both preachers and others involved in leading worship are conscious of the task ahead. The importance of the Vestry Prayer should not be under-estimated. Such prayers come in all sorts of forms. The one that goes on and on anticipating the Prayers of Intercessions in its breadth of concerns but omitting the preacher and the service about to take place is a familiar type. The prayer learned long ago but said each Sunday with a vibrant sincerity is another, as are prayers written for the occasion or read from one of a limited number of books of Vestry Prayers. Sometimes there's just the silence and the 'well shall we get on with it?' Preachers have experience of them all.

Many Church Stewards, Elders or Deacons in the Church Vestry will also admit to an equal anxiety when the moment comes to 'pray with the preacher'. They see local or lay preachers and ministers as the experts in praying and themselves as unskilled in this important moment.

At Long Street Methodist Church, Middleton, Manchester, the Stewards' Meeting explored this topic and these prayers are the result. I agreed to write a Vestry Prayer each week in addition to the prayers I produce for Sunday worship. They have been in use for eighteen months and the suggestion about publishing them came from the Church Stewards themselves.

We offer them to the wider Church because we have found them a help in the final moments we have shared each Sunday before the public Service of Worship begins. It is in that hope that we offer them to you for use in similar circumstances. May they bring glory to God, through Jesus Christ, and in the power of the Holy Spirit, and may they bring a blessing to both preachers and those who pray with them Sunday by Sunday.

John Forster, Manchester
All Souls Day 1998.

9th before Christmas

Living God, Creator of the heavens and the earth,
you have brought all things into being,
making all life possible.
You enable us to share in your creativity.
In Jesus Christ you have revealed yourself to us
and it is in his Name that we gather here today.
As we prepare to lead this act of worship
we offer ourselves to you in loving service.
May your Holy Spirit bless the preacher and people
as we join in this celebration of our faith.
Fill us with all joy in believing, we pray,
in Jesus Christ our Lord. Amen.

8th before Christmas

Blessed and holy God,
as we come together in this Act of Worship,
we turn from created things
to worship you, the Creator.
We come into the presence of our heavenly Father,
the Father of our Lord Jesus Christ.
We respond to you, Lord God;
to what you have shown yourself to be in Jesus.
Touch every life gathered here today.
Fire us all with your love
and lift us out of the ordinary and the routine.
May all who share in this sacred time
know that they have found you in Jesus. Amen.

7th before Christmas

Lord God, you have called us to this pilgrimage of faith
through Jesus Christ the Lord.
We walk with men and women of faith in the past
and those who share our faith in this present time.
You call us to this particular ministry
of preparing for and leading the worship of your people.
We bring all our preparations as an offering to you.
We come with a great sense of unworthiness
yet conscious of your call to this moment.
Bless this time together for all gathered here
and bless us too as we lead your people's praise.
We pray in the Name and Spirit of Jesus. Amen.

6th before Christmas

Almighty and eternal God,
we gather in this special moment
as we are about to lead this act of worship.
Each act of worship is special for your gathered people,
and we are conscious of the part we have to play.
As you blessed Moses in the duties you gave him,
bless us and all who share in this time together.
As you made your love real in Jesus Christ,
make your love real to us,
in us and through us, we pray.
Pour your Spirit on us who lead this act of worship,
and upon all who worship you here.
May we celebrate the Name of Jesus. Amen.

5th before Christmas

Lord God, we come into your presence
with a sense of inadequacy and unfitness
as we prepare to lead the worship of your people.
Yet Lord, you have called us to this task.
You have promised the gift of the Spirit to us.
Take our weakness and transform it with your strength.
We bring you all that has been prepared for this moment
by preacher, stewards, musicians
and your people gathered here.
Lord God, take what we bring in the Spirit,
and enable us all to worship and praise you
in love and joy, and in Jesus Christ.   Amen.

Advent One

God who comes,
come into this moment to help us and bless us.
We gather together for this act of worship:
adults and children chattering together,
organist and choir assembling
and preparing to lead our praise,
stewards at the Church doors, the sacred table,
and in the vestry making sure all is ready,
preacher bringing all that has been prepared.
Receive all that we bring, God who comes,
in this outpouring of our worship and praise.
Grace us with your presence as we gather,
the people of Jesus. Amen.

Advent Two

Word of God, spoken in the beginning;
Word made flesh in Jesus Christ;
Word of God with a human voice,
we prepare to speak your praise.
Touch every heart and voice,
mind and spirit,
in this place of worship.
May all we bring be caught up
into a harmony of love and praise.
We pray in the Spirit,
and in the Name of Jesus, the Living Word. Amen.

Advent Three

God, disturber of complacency and apathy,
you heralded the start of the ministry of Jesus
through the words and actions of John the Baptist.
Disturb our complacency and religious routine
by your powerful presence among us today.
Speak to us afresh - to people and preacher -
that we may respond to you
with new eyes, with loving hearts,
and with spirits open to your leading.
So may we worship you in all sincerity,
as we make our offering of praise,
and as we live as Christ's disciples day by day.
We ask our prayer in His Name. Amen.

Advent Four

Lord God, there is much rush and busy-ness
on this last Sunday morning before Christmas.
So many things to remember to do;
so many things crowding into our minds.
Lord God, in this precious time of quiet,
help us to focus our minds
upon what we have come to do:
to lead an act of adoration and praise;
to celebrate the coming of Jesus Christ.
Still our busy minds and our racing hearts
as we dedicate this act of worship,
and all who gather to share in it,
to you, God who comes to us in Jesus. Amen.

Christmas Eve

Emmanuel, God who comes to be with us,
we gather to begin our Christmas celebrations
here with you in Church,
gathered around the Lord's Table as your family,
as Mary and Joseph, the shepherds and kings,
gathered around your manger in Bethlehem.
We come, Lord God Emmanuel, to lead this celebration;
to lead the worship of your people on this Holy Night.
Come and meet with all who gather in this place,
and make your presence known to us,
God who comes to be with us 'as a new-born child'.
We pray in the Name of that child: 'Jesus'. Amen.

Christmas Day

Incarnate Lord, Word made flesh who dwells with us,
we come to celebrate with your people
this anniversary of your birth.
Touch us who lead this time together,
touch those who gather here with us today,
touch all who are part of our Church Family,
with the love that came down at Christmas.
So may we respond to your story with joy,
by receiving it and believing it,
and by becoming part of it ourselves
in worship and in living day by day.
We make our prayer in your Incarnate Name.   Amen.

Christmas One

Jesus Christ born among us,
this day we remember the coming of the Wise Men
who followed a Star to bring you their gifts.
We come into this place of worship to greet you:
bless your people gathered here expectantly;
bless your servants who lead this act of worship;
bless all whose gifts will enrich it.
Lord God, may this be an offering of love and praise
and a worthy response to your coming among us in Jesus.
We pray in his Name and in his Spirit.   Amen.

Christmas Two - 1

Lord God, we come to you in this Holy Season of Christmas.
We continue to celebrate the mystery of your coming in Jesus.
As we come together for this act of worship,
we remember the danger that followed your birth,
and the flight of the Holy Family into Egypt as refugees.
Incarnate Lord, you came into a real world with real dangers,
to make real the God who is with his people at all times.
As we worship you today in the same world, with all its needs,
may we be conscious of your presence with us now:
preacher and stewards, adults and children,
gathered in this offering of worship and praise.   Amen.

Christmas Two - 2

Lord Jesus Christ, in the Temple in Jerusalem
you were about your Father's business
when your anxious parents sought you out.
You were 'at home' amid the worship and devotion,
the praises and love of God's people.
Come and meet with us as we bring our worship.
Clothe us with your Spirit, we pray,
that the offering of the people,
of musicians, stewards and preacher,
may be tuned to the praises of the Living God:
Father, Son and Holy Spirit.   Amen.

Covenant Sunday

Covenant God, as we prepare to come into your presence,
we remember our heritage in the Old Covenant,
and its fulfilment in Jesus, the New Covenant.
We gather as your Methodist people
to worship you and to renew our Covenant promises.
The past year has been a mixed year for all of us,
of successes and failures, hopes and fears;
not least for us who gather
to lead your people in this service of rededication.
Clothe all who are here today with the Spirit of Jesus,
so that all that is done here
may be to your praise and glory. Amen.

Epiphany

Eternal God, through a shining star
you drew Wise Men to the manger
to worship Immanuel: God who is with us.
Your people gather here to bring their gifts
of worship and wealth, devotion and service,
to the Christ who is always among them.
We prepare ourselves - stewards and preacher -
to lead the offering of praise they bring.
Bless all that we bring, all that is done,
and grant that our gifts may be as worthy and appropriate
as were their gifts of gold, frankincense and myrrh. Amen.

Epiphany One

Incarnate Lord, we acknowledge your presence
here in this time of quiet and preparation.
You came to the river Jordan to be baptised
and John the Baptist felt you should have baptised him.
So, Lord, we feel that same sense as we come here
to speak and act in your Name today.
God used the moment of your Baptism to reveal your identity.
Use this time together today, we pray, to do the same.
Bring all that is done here into a harmony of praise.
We ask this our prayer in your most Holy Name. Amen.

Epiphany Two

Living Lord, we come together to meet you today.
We do so gladly because your words are 'life' to us.
But we also know our frailty and weakness,
and our inadequacy for the task that lays before us.
So, Lord, we take a few moments to focus upon you.
You are the One who has called us to this task.
You are the One who promises help and strength to us.
Living and loving Lord, we bring all our preparation,
we bring the faith of all who are gathered in this place.
May your Spirit help us, in all that we do here,
to make a fitting sacrifice of worship and praise.
We ask it in your Name: Jesus. Amen.

Epiphany Three

Holy One of God,
we come into your presence in awe and wonder,
for you are great and worthy to be praised.
In the presence of your holiness,
we feel unworthy, unclean and inadequate,
poorly prepared for what we gather to do.
We come here in the Name of Jesus,
knowing that you will receive the gifts we bring.
May your Spirit enrich and enable our worship,
that all of us may praise you,
with heart, mind, strength and spirit. Amen.

Epiphany Four

How can we hide our love for you,
gracious God and Father of our Lord Jesus Christ?
You have become incarnate among us
to draw forth an answering love that is visible too.
We come to Church today, in response to your love,
bringing you our adoration and our worship;
the offering of thankful and grateful people,
making our love visible as well.
Receive all that we have to offer you.
Cover the poverty of our worship, we pray,
with the generosity of your grace,
for Jesus' sake. Amen.

Epiphany Five

Lord of new beginnings,
we come before you as we have done many times before:
stewards, musicians, congregation and preacher.
Help us not to be so trapped in the familiar
that we fail to notice your surprises.
Teach us how to reach beyond our expectations
to the God who willingly waits to greet us -
whether it is here in this time of worship,
in fellowship within our Christian Family,
or in the ordinary routines of everyday life.
In all things may we follow our Lord Jesus Christ,
and live and worship through the Spirit. Amen.

9th before Easter

Lord Jesus Christ,
we are captivated by your words and teaching,
and inspired through your love in action.
Your Incarnation, your Cross and Resurrection
convince us that God is real and is with us.
We prepare to lead this act of worship in your Name,
and we offer ourselves,
that you may speak through our words and actions,
to bless all your people gathered here.
Take all that we bring to offer in your service.
Use it as a vehicle to teach your ways of love,
among this congregation and in this community.
We ask and we dare to offer in your gracious Name. Amen.

8th before Easter

Living and loving God,
in Jesus you reveal your concern
for the wholeness and well-being of each person.
Jesus, the Wounded Healer, dies and rises
to make the healing of body, mind and spirit possible.
As we come together as a worshipping community today,
Lord we bring our personal baggage
of anxieties and fears and concerns with us,
whether we are stewards or people or preacher.
Calm our anxieties with your healing peace
in these few moments of final preparation.
May we, and the whole Church Family,
feel your healing presence, and be set free
to offer you our adoration and praise,
as we gather in Jesus' saving Name.   Amen.

7th before Easter

Heavenly Father, this has been a very busy week,
with many cares and concerns to fill our thoughts.
All who gather here, preacher and stewards and people,
come into the quiet of your presence today,
and yet we are anything but quiet and peaceful.
As Jesus spoke the words: 'Peace, be still!'
to the winds and the waves to calm them,
and brought peace to his anxious disciples,
so, gracious Lord, speak your word of peace,
into our hearts and minds and spirits.
And in that peace may we offer our worship and thanksgiving
in the Spirit that was in Jesus. Amen.

Lent One

The Spirit led Jesus into the wilderness -
a place of struggle, of questioning, of temptation.
How often we share such experiences, living God:
when the sermon just won't work out;
when the things we need to do just don't fall into place;
when our prayers are formal and empty and without feeling.
Lord God, in the wilderness Jesus stands with us.
He shares our humanity, understands our frailties.
Come, meet with us, as we remember his wilderness.
Take and bless the things that we bring to offer
in this our sacrifice of worship and praise.
God who understands us - Father, Son and Holy Spirit. Amen.

Lent Two

Lord, we struggle with evil and sin
in ourselves, in the Church and in the world.
You contended with evil, indeed there were those
who accused you of being in league with evil!
You know how we fare in the struggles we engage in,
and how much we need the aid of your Spirit day by day.
We come to you as we prepare to conduct this service,
and we know that it will have its imperfections,
because we who lead it and those who share in it are flawed.
Grant your Spirit to us as we worship you,
and clothe our imperfections with your grace.
Only then can we offer all that is good and right
and holy to you, living God in Jesus.
Receive this offering of love and praise. Amen.

Lent Three

'Who do you say that I am?' was your question to Peter.
Lord, he made the great confession of faith
when he said you were the Christ, Son of the Living God.
Lord Jesus Christ, we gather together in this community,
people who make the same confession of faith.
Yet, just like Peter, we can move
from the heights to the depths in a matter of a few words.
Many words will be used in this service we are about to lead:
words sung in hymns and spoken in prayers and preaching.
Grant us the help of your Spirit,
that all our words may be worthy of your praise,
and may be a true confession of Jesus,
our Saviour and Lord.   Amen.

Lent Four

Holy God, there are many mountain-top experiences
contained within the Old and New Testaments -
and we have had such moments ourselves.
Moments that disclose your glory
and that fill us with a sense of awe and wonder.
Lord, we cannot make such moments happen to order
or demand them from you to bolster-up our faith.
We have prepared for this time of worship -
stewards, preacher and all who are gathered together -
and we pray that you will take what we offer
and use it to reveal yourself to us,
and to build us up in our Christian lives:
Holy God who reveals himself in Jesus Christ.   Amen.

Lent 5 - Passion Sunday

Gracious God, on this day we remember
the costliness of the love Jesus showed to all.
He made the ultimate sacrifice of his own life,
in order that we could glimpse the mystery of a suffering God,
whose vulnerability discloses the real power of love.
The people come into your presence with many thoughts,
the stewards have got everything ready
and the preacher is prepared to lead our worship.
Use these special moments to speak to us, we pray,
and disclose yourself to all who are gathered here:
God who suffers for us in Jesus Christ.   Amen.

Palm Sunday

Hosanna! Hosanna! Hosanna!
Blessed is he who comes in the Name of the Lord.
Holy Jesus, we would share in your recognition
as the Lord who comes to be with his people.
Those who are gathering, young and old,
are coming together to hail you and worship you,
the lowly Lord, servant of the servants of God.
Fill your people's praise with the Spirit's power,
and fulfil the hopes and prayers
of those who have prepared for this service.
May our praises be like a carpet of love
to welcome you, the Lord who comes,
as the palm branches were on the road into Jerusalem. Amen.

Maundy Thursday

Lord Jesus Christ, we gather around your table
to share the last meal with you and the disciples.
We respond to your invitation
and come to meet those you have invited with us.
Take the offering of faith and love we bring;
take the words that will be said;
take the preparation and the event itself;
take all that each one brings to your table.
Lord Jesus Christ, it is our gift of love to you.
By your presence weld it into a feast of praise;
a true celebration of Eucharist!   Amen.

Good Friday

Lord God, what a black day this is!
The day on which we remember the death of Jesus
following his crucifixion on the hill of Calvary.
This is a day of pain but also a day of hope,
sin and death are not the end but can be overcome.
Lord God, help us in this act of worship
to walk with Jesus and to stand at the foot of his Cross.
Take our pain and guilt and horror and transform them
into worship and love, into faith and hope.
We pray in the Name of our crucified Lord, Jesus. Amen.

Easter Day

Jesus Christ is risen! Hallelujah!
Risen Lord, we gather on this day of resurrection:
filled with wonder at the message given to Mary;
amazed and astonished with the disciples.
As we prepare to lead this act of praise,
let the almost unbelievable message of Easter
touch preacher, stewards and people with the joy
that comes when we grasp the glorious truth
that the Jesus who was crucified is alive!
So may we celebrate with joy,
with the whole Church of Christ,
in his Name and in his Spirit. Amen.

Easter One

Risen Lord, we come together today
as we continue to celebrate your resurrection.
We still wrestle with the mystery:
you were dead and are alive forever!
Risen Lord, as we prepare to lead this
celebration of the Easter faith,
be present with us in your risen power.
Take all that we bring, all that we are,
and use it in the worship your people offer.
We ask and offer in the Name of Jesus,
our only Saviour and risen Lord.   Amen.

Easter Two

Lord Jesus Christ, Easter demands a response.
Your resurrection is not just a brilliant ending,
but a glorious new beginning.
Things can never be the same again.
We, and all who gather here, can never be the same.
Help us to show forth the new life you give us.
Help us to do that in our worship today:
people gathering and organist playing,
preacher prepared, and stewards and choir preparing.
We come together in the Easter faith,
to celebrate the new life we are given,
through Jesus our crucified and risen Lord.
We pray in his Name and in his Spirit. Amen.

Easter Three

Living God, you reveal yourself in Jesus
and call us to a life of faith,
trusting in his words, his death and resurrection.
Lord God, we wrestle with the mystery
that is at the heart of our faith
as we gather together to worship you.
We come with our own needs, hopes, gifts and graces.
What is true of us is true of all who meet here.
Take what has been prepared for this act of praise,
Lord, may it bring you praise and glory,
and may you speak to us all through what we share together.
We pray in Jesus' Name. Amen.

Easter Four

Lord Jesus Christ, we believe:
You are the Way, the Truth, and the Life.
We gather together today - preacher and people -
to proclaim that reality in our worship.
We are your people and you are our God.
We are bound-up together in the communion of love
You have revealed to us in Jesus of Nazareth,
who calls us to make that love real in Church and world.
Receive the prayer and praise we bring in his Name,
as we offer ourselves to you in worship,
and as we dedicate ourselves in his service.   Amen.

Easter Five

Gracious God, where would we be without you?
We are fortunate you see us with the eyes of love.
You seek us as a shepherd seeks those who have wandered
away.
We are conscious of how much we fall short of your glory -
ministers and preachers, stewards and people.
Lord God, we come here today seeking to respond to you.
Receive this act of love and devotion
and lead us in your ways, we pray.
Take all the contributions to this Service -
the hidden ones and the public ones -
and receive them as an offering of our praise.
We ask it in the Name of the risen Jesus. Amen.

Ascension Day

On this day on which we celebrate your glory,
we prepare ourselves to worship you.
We pray for those who are gathering in Church,
we pray for the organist, singers and musicians,
we pray for those welcoming the congregation,
we pray for preacher and stewards gathered here.
Glorified Lord, help us to behold the mystery,
and marvel at your love revealed to us in Jesus.
May our prayer be true for all who gather here,
and for all who bring their worship and praise
on this festival of your Ascension.
We pray in your Name and in your Spirit. Amen.

Easter Six

Lord, enthroned in light and splendour,
    we come to bring you mortal praise;
    to worship you in words and music;
    in sounds and silence to adore your mystery.
    We come to offer you the highest
    and the best that we have to bring.
    Bless all who are gathering,
    preparing to focus their hearts upon you.
    Bless all that has been prepared,
    and all that will be spontaneously offered
    by preacher and people
    as they worship you
    in and through the love of Jesus. Amen.

Pentecost

Holy Spirit of God, we offer you our praise.
We seek your presence and your power
as we gather to lead this act of worship.
Touch our minds, hearts, lips with your fire
so that all that has been prepared,
and all that will be offered here today,
will carry the stamp of your presence and power.
Lead the preacher and the people:
as they meet in the Name of Jesus;
as they respond to your power and prompting;
as they approach the mystery of the living God;
as they share in this act of Christian worship. Amen.

Pentecost 1 - Trinity Sunday

Holy God, you have revealed yourself
as eternal Father, life-giving Son, and Holy Spirit.
We behold the mystery of your glory and power
as we prepare ourselves to lead your people's praise.
As we have opened ourselves to your prompting
in the preparations for this act of worship,
continue to bless us as we lead this service,
and bless the gathering congregation as well.
We respond to your love and life revealed in Jesus.
All blessing and honour be given to you,
Holy God, Father, Son and Holy Spirit.   Amen.

Pentecost 2

Living God, Father, Son and Holy Spirit,
As we gather together, in these moments before the Service
begins,
we are conscious of the imperfections in all we have to offer:
the hurried and shallow preparations
of stewards, musicians and preacher;
and the lack of preparedness and expectancy
of those who gather to worship you here.
These stand in stark contrast with your nature:
always prepared, always ready, always loving.
Lord, we offer this act of worship to you.
Clothe its imperfections with your holiness
that our love and praise may blossom as we seek
to express our love in Jesus Christ our Lord. Amen.

Pentecost 3

O Lord our God, you reign in light supreme,
and your glory fills the heavens and the earth.
In Jesus, your light shines in our darkness,
and the darkness has never put it out.
Light of God, shine upon us now,
as we prepare to enter the sanctuary
to lead your people's praise.
May your light help us to behold the glory of God.
Let the light of Christ shine in each one of us,
working through all that has been prepared for this Service;
drawing forth the adoration and worship of your people;
and enabling all to join together to express their praise.
We ask it in the Name of Jesus, our Living Lord. Amen.

Pentecost 4

Gracious God, from first to last
you are always giving of yourself to help and guide your
people.
So often in the routine of life and faith we forget this.
We are quick to praise our human achievements,
yet slow to praise your constant and unchanging love.
As we prepare to lead this sacrifice of praise,
we seek your blessing upon all who gather together
and upon all that is to be offered here in worship.
Help us, gracious God, to focus our minds on you:
the God who is closer to us than a heartbeat,
who became one with us in Jesus Christ,
and who is around us and within us in the Holy Spirit. Amen.

Pentecost 5

Glorious and Holy God, Father, Son and Holy Spirit,
you live and reign in unity supreme,
the God of earth and heaven, of time and eternity.
We prepare to approach you in this act of worship
with the Christian community gathering in this place.
Enable us to share the gifts and graces we bring:
practical or spiritual, intellectual or emotional;
regardless of age, experience or background.
May the Holy Spirit weave our offerings
into a truly loving sacrifice of praise,
in which all share in worship and receive your blessing.
We ask it in the Name of Jesus. Amen.

Pentecost 6

Living Lord, in the busy-ness of our preparation,
and the activities necessary to make this service happen,
we pause, in these last few moments, to speak to you in

prayer.

Take all that has been prepared for this moment
and clothe it with your peace.
Quieten the hearts, minds and spirits
of preacher, stewards, choir and people gathering together.
Touch us with your presence,
that we may know your nearness,
as we meet, in the Name of Jesus,
to offer you our worship.   Amen.

Pentecost 7

Lord God, there are so many demands on our time,
not least in the minutes before a service begins.
Practical things to attend to,
questions answered and problems solved.
It is so easy to forget the purpose of our meeting.
We have come to worship you,
the God who is revealed in Jesus Christ.
You are the focus of all that has been prepared.
You are the one who makes it all meaningful.
It is upon you we will build this act of worship.
You are the heart of our praise
and the focus of our love offered in Jesus' Name. Amen.

Pentecost 8

Living God, who comes to us in Jesus,
we thank you for the faith that is in us
and all those who are gathering in this place.
Living God, we come to celebrate our faith today:
in this Service we will lead on behalf of the people;
through the things prepared which we bring;
through the contributions of all who will take part;
through the spontaneous offering of adoration and worship.
May your Spirit bless each and every one,
as we meet you, as we praise you,
as we worship you, in the Name of Jesus. Amen.

Pentecost 9

Gracious and Holy God,
you never leave nor forsake your people.
You are loyal and steadfast while we are fickle.
You are always true while we waiver between opinions.
May we be conscious of your abiding presence
in these precious moments
before we go to lead the worship of this congregation.
Take all that we bring, that which we have prepared,
and use it, through the Holy Spirit,
to enable your people to reach out to you in worship.
We gather as the community of Jesus Christ
to worship in his Name and in the Spirit. Amen.

Pentecost 10

Almighty and Eternal God,
you are so generous with your gifts and blessings.
We can do nothing to deserve your love
and yet you continue to bestow it upon us all.
We gather here to worship you and to celebrate your generosity.
We bring to you our love, our gifts, our praises,
and our responses to the promptings of your Spirit.
Fuse all that we bring,
with that of those assembling in the sanctuary,
each offering and each response,
into a sacrifice of adoration and love.
We ask our prayer in the Spirit of Jesus.   Amen.

Pentecost 11

Many people are gathering in this place, Lord God.
Some are coming out of habit and routine of life,
some are coming reluctantly, others expectantly,
most bring with them cares and burdens, hopes and fears.
Lord God, all are gathering to share in this act of worship.
We have the responsibility of leading their worship
and leading them into a consciousness of your presence.
We offer to you our preparation for today,
some of it is still going on around us.
We pray that your Holy Spirit will weave all the parts together
into a seamless robe of adoration and praise,
offered to you, Lord God, in Jesus Christ. Amen.

Pentecost 12

Generous God, you have invited us into your Family
and we gather together to celebrate our life together.
We take a few moments, in the stillness and quiet,
to prepare ourselves to lead this celebration.
We thank you for your call to this ministry
and for the gifts and graces you have given
to equip us for the task before us.
Take all that we bring to this moment,
Stewards and people, musicians and preacher,
body, heart, mind and spirit together.
Here we express our love, our commitment and our worship
in our response to your generosity in Christ. Amen.

Pentecost 13

Holy and Eternal God, Father, Son and Holy Spirit,
we come together, with your people,
to give you the honour due to your great Name.
We are conscious of the inadequacy of our preparation,
and the hurry and rush
of getting to Church for many people
who are gathered here with us.
What we offer is for your praise and glory.
It is an expression of the love of your people.
Touch each one of us gathered here today with the Spirit
as we meet together to worship you
in and through Jesus Christ, our Saviour and Lord. Amen.

Pentecost 14

Wise and wonderful God, we are conscious,
in these final moments before this service begins,
that a great task lies before us
as we come to lead the worship of your people.
Bless all those who gather here to offer their praises.
Touch the hearts of all those who will take part with us.
Be with the one who has prepared for this moment,
and who will lead your people in their worship today.
We make our prayer and offer our love
in the glorious Name of Jesus, the Lord.   Amen.

Pentecost 15

Gracious and Holy God, you are the unity of your people
across the world.
As we gather together to worship you,
we come with our differences of motive and expectation,
of understanding, culture and concerns.
You are the only focus of our coming together,
for you have called us through the Lord, Jesus the Christ.
Receive and bless all that we bring to you today:
the offerings of people, stewards, musicians and preacher.
May it be a worthy vehicle
through which to bring to you our praise.   Amen.

Pentecost 16

Lord God, you love us with an everlasting love
revealed in the life and death of Jesus of Nazareth.
We come together to celebrate that wonderful love
and to seek the mercy and forgiveness you give
to those who acknowledge their faults and needs.
Meet with us, gracious God, as we gather in your presence.
Help us all to be honest and open our hearts to you.
Let your Holy Spirit work within each one,
that people and preacher may express their worship,
may offer you their adoration and praise
and know the healing of your forgiving love.
We come, we dare to ask and we pray
through Jesus, the Lord. Amen.

Pentecost 17

Many came to you during your earthly ministry, Lord,
and asked you a question, but did not want to change
in order to live out your answer.
We come to you today to bring you our worship: -
a congregation, stewards, musicians, preacher.
We come to open our hearts and minds and lives
to the light of your all-embracing love.
Help us to open our whole lives to you
and not just what we find easy or convenient.
Lead us in the Spirit, so that we may become more like you
both in our worship and our lives.   Amen.

Pentecost 18

Living God, so often when we gather here
we think we are doing you a favour,
that you should be honoured
because we can spare you the time!
In reality, it is the other way around,
like so much in your upside down Kingdom.
It is a privilege and an honour to meet in your presence:
whoever we are and whatever part we will play in this service.
Help us, Lord, to value the opportunity worship brings
to praise you for your love that never changes;
whatever our feelings or response;
and may we do it in the Spirit of Jesus. Amen.

Pentecost 19

Holy God, we prepare to enter the sanctuary
to lead the congregation in this act of worship.
We are conscious of our unworthiness
and of the rush and bustle around us.
How difficult we find it to be quiet in your presence.
It's almost as though we want to drown you out.
Forgive the lack of preparedness of all who gather.
Touch us with that healing, renewing,
transforming Spirit we see revealed in Jesus.
So may our worship be worthy of your greatness
and our lives be remade by your presence.   Amen.

Pentecost 20

All power and authority belong to you,
gracious and holy God: Father, Son and Holy Spirit.
We, your people, draw near to offer you our worship.
Touch the minds and spirits of all who are gathering,
both in Church and here in the Vestry,
with the Spirit that was in Jesus.
So may we worship you, holy and blessed God,
with minds, spirits and lives tuned to your praise
through Jesus Christ the Lord. Amen.

Pentecost 21

We prepare to approach you in this act of worship.
Some come expecting things to be done for them;
while others come prepared to give of themselves;
and we prepare ourselves to lead this service of praise.
Whatever our expectations or contributions,
take what we bring, Sovereign Lord God,
it is the offering of our love and commitment
as we respond to you through Jesus of Nazareth. Amen.

Pentecost 22

The woman at Bethany anointed you with perfume
and filled the whole house with the fragrance.
We bring the perfume of adoration and praise
as we bow in worship at your feet, Lord Christ.
May the fragrance of your presence with us
transform all the preparations and expectations
into a celebration of your life and light and love.
Touch each person present with your Spirit,
that all may be filled with your presence,
Jesus, Lord and Christ, who lives amongst us,
that the whole world may know of your glory. Amen.

Last After Pentecost

Many times in the Gospel, Jesus warns us
to be prepared to meet you in the daily round.
We come into Church today, Living God, as many times before.
Help us, church stewards and preacher,
and all who gather here with us in this place,
to know that we are in your presence;
that time and eternity are bound together in your praise.
So may we truly be a people prepared,
maintaining the common round of worship and service,
and living to your praise and glory in Jesus. Amen.

PRAYERS FOR OTHER SPECIAL DAYS

All Saints Day

Holy and blessed God,
down the ages your people have offered you their praise,
in many styles and forms, sights, smells and sounds.
Today we join the innumerable saints of God,
remembered and forgotten,
who still offer you their adoration and worship.
As we think of them, may they point us to you,
the only focus of the worship of the Body of Christ,
that we may join in the great acclamation of praise,
which springs from the whole of earth and heaven,
to celebrate your glory, through Jesus Christ. Amen.

Church Anniversary

Jesus, Lord of the Church, we are glad to be here
on this Anniversary Day of our Church in ....
This day of celebration is also a day to remember
that, without you, all this is as nothing.
So, Lord, as we prepare to lead the worship today,
fill us with your Spirit
and speak through all that is both said and done:
it is the offering of our worship and praise,
it is our thanksgiving for all that is behind,
it is our hope for your leading in the future.
May your Spirit lead our celebration today
in this offering of thanksgiving and joy. Amen.

Church Family Festival

Living Lord, God and Father of all people,
we gather together as your family in this place.
This is a day of happiness and joy
as we celebrate what your love means to us.
Bless young and old as they gather together;
bless preacher and people, stewards and musicians;
as we come to offer our worship and praise.
May your Spirit lead and guide us all
in the old and comfortable,
through the new and unfamiliar,
that in all things your praise
may be on our lips and in our hearts.
We ask it in the Name and Spirit of Jesus. Amen.

Harvest Festival

Creator God, we are surrounded by the evidence
of your bountiful provision for life in all its forms.
We come to praise you for your great goodness
to us and to all that you have created.
Bless us in our celebration of your bounty,
not least for your coming among us in Jesus of Nazareth.
Touch all who are gathered in this Church today.
Receive the response of praise and thanksgiving,
from young and old, from adults and children.
May it be sincerely and lovingly offered
as we worship you and bless you in Jesus' Name. Amen.

Home Mission Sunday

Lord God, Parent and Saviour, Lord and Friend,
today we focus on the mission you entrust to us:
a mission to the community inside and outside the Church.
Open our ears and eyes, minds, hearts and spirits,
that we may hear you speaking to us,
and calling us to your service.
Bless with your Spirit all who gather together
to offer you their worship today.
Use the familiar to challenge us with your call:
preacher and people, stewards and musicians,
that all may respond in faith and hope and love. Amen.

Ministries Sunday

Gracious and Holy God, through the Spirit
you give gifts to each one of your servants.
In this service,
help us to harness all the gifts you have given
into the offering of our worship and praise.
May this time of worship and fellowship together
be an expression of the offering of our lives,
as we each exercise the ministry you give to us,
and respond to your call in Jesus Christ. Amen.

Remembrance Sunday

As we prepare to come into your presence,
gracious and loving God,
on this day of remembering,
we seek your blessing for all who gather here today.
Send your Holy Spirit upon us,
as we meet in the Name of Jesus of Nazareth.
Touch all our hearts with your love:
that we may freely offer you our praises;
that we may rise above our inadequacies;
that our worship may be an expression of our love.
As we remember the sacrifices of the past,
help us to build a future of justice and peace.   Amen.

Social Responsibility Sunday

Jesus calls us to be his disciples
and live out our faith in the daily round of life;
that our worship may always be rooted in love in action.
On this Social Responsibility Sunday,
help those of us who prepare to lead this service,
that your people's worship may not be divorced from life,
and that love expressed to God in praise
may find its expression in love of self and neighbour,
and so fulfil our Lord's command.
We pray in his Name and in the Spirit.   Amen.

Wesley Day

Living God, you have brought forth the Methodist People
through the ministry of John and Charles Wesley.
With Methodists all over the world,
we prepare ourselves to come into your sanctuary;
we worship you in word and in music;
in praise and fellowship and social concern.
Rekindle in us that zeal for your Good News
that warmth of fellowship and concern,
that openness to you, our neighbour and each other,
as we celebrate our heritage of faith,
through Jesus Christ our Lord. Amen.

World Church Sunday

Creator God, you have set us in a wonderful world;
a world of diversity and beauty and splendour.
On World Church Sunday we celebrate
how this is expressed in the people of God;
in the limbs and organs of the Body of Christ;
through the sounds and actions of the family of God.
We praise you for this rich diversity,
through which your Name is worshipped and glorified
by every race and language and tongue.
May we make our contribution to this festival of your praise,
as we bring you our worship,
now offered to you in Jesus' Name. Amen.

A Youth Service

Lord, this will be a service with a difference!
Different sights and sounds and actions
expressing your praise with a modern beat.
Yet young and old are gathering together
to make praise and to offer worship together.
As you crossed the boundaries of age and culture,
speaking to young and old, female and male,
so we seek your presence here with us today.
Bless all the preparation and activity
as we make our act of praise real.
Touch all who take part, and all who share together,
joining together and offering you their worship.
We pray in the Name and Spirit of Jesus. Amen.

New Year's Eve

Eternal Father, living Son and indwelling Spirit,
the old year draws towards its final moments,
and we stand on the threshold of the New Year ahead.
We thank you for the fellowship we have shared,
in leading the worship of the people of God
during the last year.
Meet with us again in these final moments of preparation.
Touch us with your Spirit and bless your gathered family
as we prepare to enter the New Year in your presence.
We pray in the precious Name of Jesus. Amen.

Eve of the Millennium

God who came to be with us in Jesus,
we prepare to lead the worship of your people
as the second Millennium draws to a close:
the 2000th anniversary of your Incarnation.
We are conscious, with all who have gone before us,
of our frailty in the face of your eternity;
of our sinfulness before your holiness;
as we seek to express our love for you.
Lord, may all who gather in this place tonight
be conscious of your presence –
people, preacher, stewards and musicians -
at this special moment in human time and history.
We meet with the Body of Christ world-wide,
to offer you our millennial praise, in Jesus's Name,
and in the power of the Holy Spirit. Amen.

First Sunday of the Third Millennium

Gracious and Holy God,
You have acted in time and history down the centuries
and revealed yourself through men and women
who disclosed your truth and acted in your name.
Over the last two thousand years
You have revealed yourself in Jesus:
God made man, crucified and risen, ascended and glorified.
In this first offering of worship of the Third Millennium
we seek to offer all that is the highest and best
from people and preacher, church musicians and leaders,
as we gather in the Name of Jesus and in the Spirit.
All praise be to you, Gracious and Holy God,
throughout all the ages and for all eternity. Amen.

MOORLEY'S

are growing Publishers, adding several new titles to our list each year. We also undertake private publications and commissioned works.

Our range of publications
Includes: **Books of Verse**
Devotional Poetry
Recitations
Drama
Bible Plays
Sketches
Nativity Plays
Passiontide Plays
Easter Plays
Demonstrations
Resource Books
Assembly Material
Songs & Musicals
Children's Addresses
Prayers & Graces
Daily Readings
Books for Speakers
Activity Books
Quizzes
Puzzles
Painting Books
Daily Readings
Church Stationery
Notice Books
Cradle Rolls
Hymn Board Numbers

Please send a S.A.E. (approx 9" x 6") for the current catalogue or consult your local Christian Bookshop who should stock or be able to order our titles.